I0775965

THE BAHAMAS 2016 HUMAN RIGHTS REPORT

EXECUTIVE SUMMARY

The Commonwealth of the Bahamas is a constitutional, parliamentary democracy. Prime Minister Perry Christie's Progressive Liberal Party won control of the government in May 2012 elections that international observers found generally free and fair.

Civilian authorities maintained effective control over the security forces.

The most serious human rights problems included mistreatment of irregular migrants, an inefficient judicial system, and the perception of impunity on the part of law enforcement and immigration officials accused of using excessive force.

Other human rights problems included: violence against prisoners in detention facilities; substandard detention conditions, including poor nutrition; corruption; inhibition of free speech through criminal libel laws; government intimidation of nongovernmental organizations; violence and discrimination against women; sexual abuse of children; and discrimination based on ethnic descent, sexual orientation, or HIV status.

The government took action in some cases against police officers and other officials accused of abuse of power.

Section 1. Respect for the Integrity of the Person, Including Freedom from:

a. Arbitrary Deprivation of Life and other Unlawful or Politically Motivated Killings

There were no reports that the government or its agents committed arbitrary or unlawful killings, although there were occasional reports of fatal shootings and questionable deaths of suspects in police custody. Bystanders at some shootings claimed that police were too quick to use their firearms and declared that in some instances police officers acted unprofessionally.

Authorities reported seven fatalities in police operations during the year; in each case the government reported the suspect was armed.

In August 2015 family members and some other witnesses reported that police officers shot and killed a suspect who was lying on the ground with his hands in the air. Police officials promised a full investigation of the allegations but stated they did not believe the allegations were credible. The case remained pending as of December.

b. Disappearance

There were no reports of politically motivated disappearances.

c. Torture and Other Cruel, Inhuman, or Degrading Treatment or Punishment

The constitution prohibits torture and cruel, inhuman, or degrading treatment or punishment. At times citizens and visitors alleged instances of police abuse of criminal suspects.

On July 8, a foreign citizen reported he had been beaten by two or more corrections officers at the Bahamas Department of Corrections (BDOC). He said that following an altercation with an inmate, prison guards placed him in handcuffs, bent him over a cart, beat him with a PVC plumbing pipe wrapped in duct tape, and then took him back to his cell without providing any medical attention.

A migrant held in the immigration detention center in Freeport alleged unprompted, regular beatings from the guards, as well as inappropriate sexual behavior toward female detainees.

Prison and Detention Center Conditions

Prison and detention center conditions failed to meet international standards in some areas, and conditions at the government's only prison remained harsh due to overcrowding.

Physical Conditions: Overcrowding, poor sanitation, and inadequate access to medical care remained problems in the men's maximum-security block. In October 2015 the commissioner of corrections reported the maximum-security block of the prison held 625 inmates in spaces designed to hold approximately 375 inmates when constructed in 1953. The minister of national security reported that the BDOC, which was originally built to hold 1,000 prisoners, held 1,727 inmates as of October 2016.

Inmates reported receiving only two meals per day, and often only one, with a meal sometimes consisting only of bread and tea. Fresh fruit and vegetables were rare to nonexistent. Prisoners also reported infrequent access to drinking water and inability to save potable water due to lack of storage containers for the prisoners. A few cells also lacked running water, and in those cells, inmates removed human waste by bucket.

Prison guards complained about the lack of a full-time dentist and a failure to appoint a staff psychiatrist.

There were four inmate deaths through October 2015, reportedly due to HIV infection, natural causes, an apparent suicide, and injuries resulting from fighting. Reports from the coroner's court were pending on the latter two deaths. The government did not provide updated statistics in 2016.

In August 2016, upon the conclusion of a Royal Bahamas Defense Force (RBDF) hearing that was closed to the public, the Bahamian government cleared five RBDF marines accused of beating five Cuban detainees at the CRDC in 2013.

Administration: The BDOC stated that prisoner complaints generally related to pretrial detention duration, heat in cells, untimely medical care, food quality, and untimely cleaning of bedding materials and/or clothing. Through October 1, authorities reported 717 preliminary inquiries and investigations of staff and inmates. An independent authority does not exist to investigate credible allegations of inhuman conditions.

Migrant detainees did not have access to an ombudsman or other means of submitting uncensored complaints, except through their national embassy or consulate.

Independent Monitoring: Human rights organizations complained that the government did not consistently grant requests by independent human rights observers for access to the BDOC facility, the CRDC, and the two juvenile centers. The government maintained additional bureaucratic procedures for some civil society organizations to gain access to the detention center, making it difficult to visit detainees on a regular basis. The government denied multiple official requests for consular access to the CRDC to assess conditions.

d. Arbitrary Arrest or Detention

The constitution prohibits arbitrary arrest and detention, and the government generally observed these prohibitions, with the exception of immigration raids.

Numerous Haitian migrants reported being detained by immigration officials and solicited for bribes of one thousand to three thousand Bahamian dollars (B$) ($1,000-$3,000) (one B$=one U.S. dollar), with the CRDC front office functioning as a clearinghouse. Many claimed that immigration officers targeted their dwellings once their undocumented status was discovered, demanding multiple bribes. Haitian migrants and civil society organizations complained of frequent warrantless searches of Haitian homes without probable cause.

Government officials reported that immigrant detainees who presented a security risk were held at the BDOC facility. In February the Supreme Court ordered the release of two Cuban men who had been detained for almost three years without criminal charges. The government had stated that release of the individuals posed a potential security risk and that it had actively sought a third country for resettlement, as their country of nationality refused to accept their return.

Role of the Police and Security Apparatus

The Royal Bahamas Police Force (RBPF) maintains internal security. The small RBDF is primarily responsible for external security but also provides security at the CRDC and performs some domestic security functions such as guarding foreign embassies. The Ministry of National Security oversees both the RBPF and the RBDF. The RBDF augments the RBPF in administrative and support roles.

Authorities automatically placed under investigation police officers involved in shooting or killing a suspect. Police investigated all cases of police shootings and deaths in police custody and referred them to a coroner's court for further evaluation. The Police Complaints and Corruption Branch, which reports directly to the deputy commissioner, is responsible for investigating allegations of police brutality or other abuse.

In addition to the Complaints and Corruption Branch, the independent Police Complaints Inspectorate Office investigated complaints against police, but the government did not provide updated statistics in 2016.

From January to October 2015, 157 complaints were lodged with the Complaints and Corruption Branch, with assault, damage, and unlawful arrest the most frequent categories of grievance. The government did not provide updated statistics in 2016. According to the Ministry of National Security, authorities resolved 103 of these through investigation "that may result in internal discipline, counseling with complainant and accused, compensation, or advisement." The ministry reported referring no cases to the Magistrate's Court for prosecution. The RBPF took action against police misconduct, firing multiple officers during the year for illegal activities, including two officers convicted of stealing $22,000 during a traffic stop.

Arrest Procedures and Treatment of Detainees

Authorities generally conducted arrests openly and, when required, obtained judicially issued warrants. Serious cases, including suspected narcotics or firearms offenses, do not require warrants where probable cause exists. The law provides that authorities must charge a suspect within 48 hours of arrest. Arrested persons must appear before a magistrate within 48 hours (or by the next business day for cases arising on weekends and holidays) to hear the charges against them, although some persons on remand claimed they were not brought before a magistrate within the 48-hour period. Police may apply for a 48-hour extension upon simple request to the court and for longer extensions with sufficient showing of need. The government generally respected the right to a judicial determination of the legality of arrests. The constitution provides the right for those arrested or detained to retain an attorney at their own expense; volunteer legal aides were sometimes available. Minors under age 18 are provided legal assistance only when they are charged under offenses before the Supreme Court; otherwise, there is no official representation of minors before the courts.

There is a functioning bail system, although arrestees often waited up to two years before receiving bail. Individuals who could not post bail were held on remand until they faced trial. Judges sometimes authorized cash bail for foreigners arrested on minor charges; however, foreign suspects generally preferred to plead guilty and pay a fine rather than pursue their right to defend themselves, in view of possible delays in court cases and harsh conditions in prison.

Pretrial Detention: Attorneys and other prisoner advocates continued to complain of excessive pretrial detention due to the failure of the criminal justice system to try even the most serious cases in a timely manner. The constitution provides that authorities may hold suspects in pretrial detention for a "reasonable period of time," which was defined as two years. As of October 2015, 411 prisoners, including 27 non-Bahamian citizens, were awaiting trial. The government did not provide updated statistics in 2016. Authorities used an electronic ankle-bracelet surveillance system in which they released selected suspects awaiting trial with an ankle bracelet on the understanding that the person would adhere to strict and person-specific guidelines defining allowable movement within the country.

Authorities detained irregular immigrants, primarily Haitians, until arrangements could be made for them to leave the country or they obtained legal status. The average length of detention varied significantly by nationality, willingness of governments to accept their nationals back in a timely manner, and availability of funds to pay for repatriation. Authorities usually repatriated Haitians within one to two weeks. In a 2014 agreement between the governments of the Bahamas and Haiti, the government of Haiti agreed to accept the return of its nationals without undue delay, and both governments agreed that Haitian migrants found on vessels illegally in Bahamian territorial waters would be subject to immediate repatriation. In return the Bahamian government agreed to continue reviewing the status of Haitian nationals with no legal status and without criminal records who either had arrived in the Bahamas before January 1985 or had resided continuously in the Bahamas since that time. Authorities held irregular immigrants convicted of crimes other than immigration violations at the BDOC facility where, after serving their sentences, they often remained for weeks or months pending deportation.

The government continued to enforce the 2014 immigration policy that clarified requirements for non-Bahamian citizens to carry the passport of their nationality and proof of legal status in the country. Some international organizations alleged that enforcement focused primarily on individuals of Haitian origin, that rights of children were not respected, and that expedited deportations did not allow time for due process. There were also widespread, credible reports that immigration officials physically abused persons as they were being detained and that officials solicited and accepted bribes to avoid detention or secure release.

Activists for the Haitian community acknowledged that few formal complaints were filed with government authorities because of these allegations, which they attributed to a widespread perception of impunity for police and immigration authorities and fear of reprisal among minority communities. The government denied these allegations and publicly committed to carry out immigration operations with due respect for internationally accepted human rights standards, including the involvement of the Ministry of Social Services, where warranted, in cases involving children, scaled enforcement based on the ability to provide adequate housing for detainees, and full investigations of any allegations of abuse.

<u>Detainee's Ability to Challenge Lawfulness of Detention before a Court</u>: Persons arrested or detained, whether on criminal or other grounds, are entitled to challenge in court the legal basis or arbitrary nature of their detention, although this process sometimes took several years.

e. Denial of Fair Public Trial

Although the constitution provides for an independent judiciary, sitting judges are not granted tenure, and some law professionals asserted that judges were incapable of rendering completely independent decisions due to lack of job security. Procedural shortcomings and trial delays were a problem. The courts were unable to keep pace with the rise in criminal cases, and there was a growing backlog.

Trial Procedures

Defendants enjoy the right to a presumption of innocence until proven guilty, to be informed promptly and in detail of the charges, to a fair and free public trial without undue delay, to be present at their trial, to have adequate time and facilities to prepare a defense, to receive free interpretation as necessary from the moment charged through all appeals, and to present their own witnesses and evidence. Although defendants generally have the right to access government-held evidence and confront adverse witnesses, in some cases the law allows witnesses to testify anonymously against accused perpetrators in order to protect themselves from intimidation or retribution. Authorities frequently dismissed serious charges because witnesses either refused to testify or could not be located. Defendants also have a right not to be compelled to testify or confess guilt and to appeal. The law extends these rights to all defendants.

Defendants may hire an attorney of their choice. The government provided legal representation only to destitute suspects charged with capital crimes, leaving large numbers of defendants without adequate legal representation. Lack of representation contributed to excessive pretrial detention, as some accused lacked the means to pursue their cases toward trial.

A large number of juvenile offenders appear in court with court-appointed guardians ad litem. A conflict arises when the magistrate requests "information" about a child's background and requests that the same social worker prepare a probation report. The Department of Social Services prepares the report, which includes a recommendation on the eventual sentence for the child. In essence the government-assigned social worker tasked with protecting and safeguarding the welfare of the child is the same individual tasked with writing the report to the judge recommending the appropriate punishment for the child.

A significant backlog of cases awaiting trial remained a problem. Delays reportedly lasted five years or more, although the government increased the number of criminal courts and continued working to clear the backlog. Once cases went to trial, they were often further delayed due to poor case and court management, such as inaccurate handling or presentation of evidence and inaccurate scheduling of witnesses, jury members, and accused criminals for testimony.

Local legal professionals also attributed delays to a variety of longstanding systemic problems, such as slow and limited police investigations, inefficient prosecution strategies, limited forensic capacity, lengthy legal procedures, and staff shortages in the Prosecutor's Office and the courts.

Political Prisoners and Detainees

There were no reports of political prisoners or detainees.

Civil Judicial Procedures and Remedies

There is an independent and impartial judiciary in civil matters, and there is access to a court to bring lawsuits seeking damages for, or cessation of, human rights violations.

f. Arbitrary or Unlawful Interference with Privacy, Family, Home, or Correspondence

The constitution prohibits such actions, and the government generally respected these prohibitions; however, in migrant villages witnesses reported immigration officers' habitual warrantless entry of homes without probable cause.

While the law usually requires a court order for entry into or search of a private residence, a police inspector or more senior police official may authorize a search without a court order where probable cause to suspect a weapons violation or drug possession exists.

Section 2. Respect for Civil Liberties, Including:

a. Freedom of Speech and Press

The constitution provides for freedom of speech and press, and the government generally respected these rights. An independent press; a relatively effective-- albeit extremely backlogged--judiciary; and a functioning democratic political system combined to promote freedom of speech and press. Independent media were active and expressed a wide variety of views without significant restriction.

Freedom of Speech and Expression: In response to criticism of the government's immigration policy that took effect in 2014, the Ministry of Foreign Affairs and Immigration reminded citizens that the Bahamas Nationality Act allows the foreign minister, who is the minister responsible for nationality and citizenship, to revoke citizenship from a person who "has shown himself by act or speech to be disloyal or disaffected towards the Bahamas." In August 2015 the foreign minister threatened to revoke the permanent residency status of a critic of the government.

Libel/Slander Laws: The law criminalizes both negligent and intentional libel, with a penalty of six months' imprisonment for the former and two years for the latter. Although the International Press Institute called on the government to begin reform and elimination of criminal defamation laws, the government increased its use of libel laws during the year. In August the government arrested two men for a rap song that attacked Prime Minister Christie in explicit language, held them for 36 hours before release, and continued to investigate them for criminal libel. One of the detainees was an outspoken activist frequently critical of the Christie administration. In September authorities arrested a lawyer on criminal libel charges for "defamatory statements" intended "to injure and expose" senior police officials to "general hatred, contempt, or ridicule."

Internet Freedom

The government did not restrict access to the internet or censor online content, and there were no credible reports that the government monitored private online communications without appropriate legal authorization. The internet was widely available on New Providence and Grand Bahama islands, and the International Telecommunication Union estimated that 78 percent of the population used the internet during the year.

Academic Freedom and Cultural Events

There were no government restrictions on academic freedom or cultural events. The Plays and Films Control Board rated and censored plays and films for public viewing.

b. Freedom of Peaceful Assembly and Association

Freedom of Association

The constitution provides for freedom of assembly and association, and the government generally respected these rights, although the climate for civil society groups appeared to be worsening. Civil rights organizations protesting the government's immigration enforcement policy and an environmental organization credibly alleged that some government officials sought to constrain their freedom of speech and association rights by publicly labeling the groups as traitors and refusing to conduct adequate investigations of or provide police protection from threats. Cabinet members also sought to intimidate a local environmental group by reading its hacked e-mails and financial information from the floor of Parliament, accusing the group of attempting to overthrow the ruling political party. The Inter-American Commission on Human Rights requested the government to undertake precautionary measures to protect six members of the environmental group following reported threats against their lives and personal integrity "as a result of their work as human rights defenders." An activist with a reform-oriented organization claimed police questioned him for his activities. He also stated that the government warned clients away from his business. Police reportedly investigated the background of a judge who ruled in favor of a human rights nongovernmental organization (NGO).

c. Freedom of Religion

See the Department of State's *International Religious Freedom Report* at www.state.gov/religiousfreedomreport/.

d. Freedom of Movement, Internally Displaced Persons, Protection of Refugees, and Stateless Persons

The constitution provides for freedom of internal movement, foreign travel, emigration, and repatriation, and the government generally respected these rights. The government generally cooperated with the Office of the UN High

Commissioner for Refugees (UNHCR) and other humanitarian organizations in assisting refugees and asylum seekers.

Protection of Refugees

Access to Asylum: According to the government, trained individuals screened applicants for asylum and referred them to the Immigration Department of the Ministry of Foreign Affairs and Immigration for further review. Government procedure requires that the ministry forward approved applications to the cabinet for a final decision on granting or denying asylum. Throughout the year the government worked to develop institutionalized asylum procedures to enhance the processing of asylum seekers and refugees. Authorities did not systematically involve UNHCR in asylum proceedings, but they did seek advice on specific cases during the year and granted UNHCR access to interview some detained asylum seekers awaiting deportation.

Refoulement: In 2013 the government signed an agreement with the government of Cuba to expedite removal of detainees. The announced intent of this agreement was to reduce the amount of time Cuban migrants spent in detention; however, concerns persisted that it also allowed for information sharing that heightened the risk of persecution of detainees and their families.

Stateless Persons

The government did not effectively implement laws and policies to provide certain habitual residents the opportunity to gain nationality in a timely manner and on a nondiscriminatory basis. Children born in the country to non-Bahamian parents, to an unwed Bahamian father and a non-Bahamian mother, or outside the country to a Bahamian mother and a non-Bahamian father do not acquire citizenship at birth.

Bahamian-born persons of foreign heritage must apply for citizenship during a 12-month window following their 18th birthday, sometimes waiting many years for a government response. The narrow window for application, difficult documentary requirements, and long waiting times left multiple generations without a confirmed nationality. These restrictions primarily affected those of Haitian descent.

There were no reliable estimates of the number of persons without a confirmed nationality. The government asserted that a number of "stateless" individuals had a legitimate claim to Haitian citizenship but refused to pursue it due to fear of deportation or loss of future claim to Bahamian citizenship. Such persons often faced waiting periods of several years for the government to decide on their nationality applications and, as a result, lacked proper documentation to secure employment, housing, access to health services, and other public facilities.

Individuals born in the country to non-Bahamian parents were eligible to apply for "Belonger" status that entitled them to work, access to public high school-level education, and a fee-for-service health-care insurance program. After significant delay, hundreds of Belonger permits were issued during the year. Human rights advocates criticized the health insurance program as having unrealistic payment requirements that limited widespread access. Authorities allowed individuals born in the country to non-Bahamian parents to pay the tuition rate for Bahamian students when enrolled in college and while waiting for their request for citizenship to be processed. To attend government primary and secondary schools, the Ministry of Education requires students to have a student permit or a passport with residency stamp. Community leaders reported that many irregular migrant children, as well as children born in the Bahamas to irregular migrant parents, were barred from attending classes.

Section 3. Freedom to Participate in the Political Process

The constitution and laws provide citizens the ability to choose their government in free and fair periodic elections held by secret ballot and based on universal and equal suffrage.

Elections and Political Participation

Recent Elections: Prime Minister Perry Christie took office after his opposition Progressive Liberal Party (PLP) defeated the Free National Movement (FNM) in a general election in 2012. The PLP won 29 of the 38 parliamentary seats, with 48 percent of the popular vote. The FNM won the remaining nine seats. Election observers from the Organization of American States and foreign embassies found the elections to be generally free and fair.

Participation of Women and Minorities: No laws limit the participation of women and minorities in the political process, and women and minorities did participate. Seven members of parliament and the governor general were women. Four members of parliament were minorities, but minorities were unrepresented in the cabinet.

Section 4. Corruption and Lack of Transparency in Government

The law provides criminal penalties for corruption by officials; however, the government did not implement the law effectively, and officials engaged in corrupt practices with impunity. There were frequent reports of government corruption during the year.

Corruption: The procurement process was particularly susceptible to corruption, as it is opaque, contains no requirement to engage in open public tenders, and does not allow review of award decisions. In May a former state energy-company board member was convicted under the Prevention of Bribery Act, the first significant case brought under the act since 1989. In July he was sentenced to pay a fine of $14,000 and to make a payment of $221,000, equal to the amount of the bribe, within nine months to the electric company; the court determined that the noncustodial sentence was appropriate due to his ill health.

Financial Disclosure: The Public Disclosure Act requires senior public officials, including senators and members of parliament, to declare their assets, income, and liabilities on an annual basis. The government publishes a summary of the individual declarations. There is no independent verification of the submitted data, and the rate of annual submission was weak, except in election years.

Public Access to Information: As of October the government, which had not issued implementing regulations to bring the 2012 Freedom of Information Act into force, announced plans to repeal and replace the act.

Section 5. Governmental Attitude Regarding International and Nongovernmental Investigation of Alleged Violations of Human Rights

A number of international human rights organizations operated without government restriction, investigating and publishing their findings on human rights cases, although the government was less cooperative with domestic organizations.

Government Human Rights Bodies: A governmental commissioner with ombudsman-like duties enjoyed the government's cooperation and was considered effective.

Section 6. Discrimination, Societal Abuses, and Trafficking in Persons

Women

<u>Rape and Domestic Violence</u>: Rape is illegal, but the law does not protect against spousal rape, except if the couple is separated, in the process of divorce, or if there is a restraining order in place. The maximum penalty for an initial rape conviction is seven years; the maximum for subsequent rape convictions is life imprisonment. In practice, however, the maximum sentence was 14 years' imprisonment.

Violence against women continued to be a serious, widespread problem. The 2015 Strategic Plan to Address Gender-Based Violence reported a total of 2,390 incidences of sexual offenses, including rape, attempted rape, unlawful sexual intercourse, incest, and other sexual offenses, between 2003 and 2013.

The law recognizes domestic violence as a crime separate from assault and battery, and the government generally enforced the law, although women's rights groups cited some reluctance on the part of law enforcement authorities to intervene in domestic disputes. The Bahamas Crisis Center (BCC) worked with police by providing them with a counselor referral service when encountering rape victims. The BCC operated a toll-free hotline in New Providence and Grand Bahama, run by trained volunteers to respond to emergency calls 24 hours a day. Governmental and private women's organizations continued public awareness campaigns, highlighting the problems of abuse and domestic violence. The Ministry of Social Services and Community Development's Department of Social Services, in partnership with a private organization, operated a safe house to assist female survivors. In November the Bureau of Women's Affairs became the Department of Gender and Family Affairs and increased its staffing. The department was reasonably well funded and received grant funding from UN Women for special projects.

<u>Sexual Harassment</u>: The law prohibits criminal "quid pro quo" sexual harassment and authorizes penalties of up to $5,000 and a maximum of two years' imprisonment. There were no official reports of workplace sexual harassment during the year. Civil rights advocates complained that criminal prohibitions were not enforced effectively and asserted that civil remedies were needed, including a prohibition on "hostile environment" sexual harassment.

<u>Reproductive Rights</u>: Couples and individuals generally have the right to decide the number, spacing, and timing of their children; manage their reproductive health; and have access to the information and means to do so, free from discrimination, coercion, or violence.

<u>Discrimination</u>: The law does not prohibit discrimination based on gender, and a constitutional referendum on gender equality, including prohibition of discrimination on the basis of sex, was soundly defeated in June. Women with foreign-born spouses do not have the same right as men to transmit citizenship to their spouse or children (see section 2.d., Statelessness).

Women were generally free of economic discrimination, and the law provides for equal pay for equal work. The law also provides for the same legal status and rights for women as for men; however, women reported that it was more difficult for them to qualify for credit and to own a business.

Children

<u>Birth Registration</u>: Children born in the country to married parents, one of whom is Bahamian, acquire citizenship at birth. Those born to non-Bahamian parents, to an unwed Bahamian father and a non-Bahamian mother, or outside the country to a Bahamian mother and a non-Bahamian father do not automatically acquire citizenship. In the case of unwed parents, the child takes the citizenship of the mother. A constitutional referendum to equalize citizenship transmission for men and women was defeated in June. All children born in the country may apply for citizenship upon reaching their 18th birthday. There is universal birth registration, and all births must be registered within 21 days of delivery.

<u>Child Abuse</u>: Child abuse and neglect remained serious problems. The RBPF operated a hotline regarding missing or exploited children. The law provides severe penalties for child abuse and requires all persons having contact with a child they believe has been physically or sexually abused to report their suspicions to the police.

The penalties for rape of a minor are the same as those for rape of an adult. While a victim's consent is insufficient defense against allegations of statutory rape, it is sufficient defense if an individual can demonstrate that the accused had "reasonable cause to believe that the victim was above 16 years of age," provided the accused was under age 18.

Sexual exploitation of children through incestuous relationships occasionally occurred, and anecdotal reports continued to suggest that this was a particular problem outside Nassau. The Ministry of Social Services may remove children from abusive situations if a court deems it necessary. The ministry provided services to abused and neglected children through a public-private center for children, the public hospital family-violence program, and the BCC.

Early and Forced Marriage: The legal minimum age for marriage is 18, although minors may marry at 15 with parental permission.

Sexual Exploitation of Children: The minimum age for consensual sex is 16 years. The law considers any association or exposure of a child to prostitution or a prostitution house as cruelty, neglect, or mistreatment of a child. Additionally, the offense of having sex with a minor carries a penalty of life imprisonment. Child pornography is against the law. A person who produces it is liable to life imprisonment; dissemination or possession of it calls for a penalty of 20 years' imprisonment.

Institutionalized Children: Children as young as 10 years old can be charged as an adult or a juvenile before a criminal court. First-time juvenile offenders charged with nonviolent or lesser offenses faced detention and custodial sentences at the Simpson Penn School for Boys, Willie Mae Pratt Center for Girls, or the BDOC facility.

When a juvenile is arrested and taken into custody, if authorities are unable to contact a parent or guardian, police call in a social worker as a de facto parent. There was no protection to prevent juveniles from being shackled to, or transported with, adult offenders. The BDOC maintained a juvenile area at the prison facility; however, there was no strict enforcement of the sight/sound separation of juvenile and adult inmates.

International Child Abductions: The country is a party to the 1980 Hague Convention on the Civil Aspects of International Child Abduction. See the Department of State's *Annual Report on International Parental Child Abduction* at travel.state.gov/content/childabduction/en/legal/compliance.html.

Anti-Semitism

The local Jewish community numbered approximately 300 persons. There were no reports of anti-Semitic acts.

Trafficking in Persons

See the Department of State's *Trafficking in Persons Report* at
www.state.gov/j/tip/rls/tiprpt/.

Persons with Disabilities

In 2015 the government passed the implementing legislation for the 2014 Persons
with Disabilities Act. The law prohibits discrimination in employment, education,
the judicial system, health care, and access, and it gives businesses and public
buildings two years to make needed access improvements. Although the previous
law mandated access for persons with physical disabilities in new public buildings,
authorities rarely enforced this requirement, and very few buildings and public
facilities were accessible to persons with disabilities. The Education Act affords
equal access for students, but only as resources permit, with this decision made by
individual schools. On less-populated islands, children with learning disabilities
often sat disengaged in the back of classrooms because resources were not
available. Other legislation prohibits discrimination based on disability.

A mix of government and private residential and nonresidential institutions
provided education, training, counseling, and job placement services for adults and
children with disabilities.

National/Racial/Ethnic Minorities

The country's racial and ethnic groups generally coexisted peacefully, but anti-
Haitian prejudice and resentment regarding Haitian immigration was widespread.
According to unofficial estimates, between 40,000 and 80,000 residents were
Haitians or persons of Haitian descent, making them the largest ethnic minority.
Many persons of Haitian origin lived in shantytowns with limited sewage and
garbage services, law enforcement, or other infrastructure. For example, a number
of shantytowns on New Providence and other islands consisted of houses built
from trash and discarded building materials, with few organizational,
infrastructure, or sanitation measures in place. The government occasionally
evicted residents and demolished some settlements due to health and safety
concerns. Fires frequently broke out in Haitian shantytowns in Nassau, at least
some of which were deliberately set, according to human rights organizations.
Authorities generally granted Haitian children access to education and social
services, but interethnic tensions and inequities persisted. Haitians generally had
difficulty in securing citizenship, residence, or work permits.

In 2014 the government began conducting large-scale immigration raids in Haitian neighborhoods and increased deportations of Haitian immigrants. Members of the community, as well as human rights NGOs, argued that the raids were conducted without probable cause and were marked by verbal and physical abuse. An elderly, bedridden woman claimed that immigration officers stomped and kicked her in October, hospitalizing her for 15 days and rendering her permanently unable to walk. Witnesses also claimed that warrantless searches of homes were common during these raids.

Members of the Haitian community complained of discrimination in the job market, specifically employers seeking advantage by threat of deportation controlled identity and work-permit documents.

Acts of Violence, Discrimination, and Other Abuses Based on Sexual Orientation and Gender Identity

Activists reported that societal discrimination against lesbian, gay, bisexual, transgender, and intersex (LGBTI) individuals occurred, with some persons claiming job and housing discrimination based on sexual orientation. Victims had no legal recourse, as the law provides no protection from such discrimination. Although sexual activity between same-sex consenting adults is legal, the law defines the age of consent for same-sex couples as 18, compared with 16 for heterosexual couples.

Activists reported that LGBTI individuals rarely reported abuse to authorities, often because of reluctance to reveal their sexual orientation rather than from fear of police harassment.

HIV and AIDS Social Stigma

Stigma and employment discrimination against persons with HIV/AIDS were high, but there were no reports of violence against persons with HIV/AIDS. The law prohibits discrimination in employment based on HIV/AIDS status. Children with HIV/AIDS also faced discrimination, and authorities often did not tell teachers that a child was HIV positive due to fear of verbal abuse from both educators and peers. The government maintained a home for orphaned children infected with HIV/AIDS.

Section 7. Worker Rights

a. Freedom of Association and the Right to Collective Bargaining

The law provides for the right of workers to form and join independent unions, participate in collective bargaining, and conduct legal strikes. The law prohibits antiunion discrimination. By law employers can be compelled to reinstate workers illegally fired for union activity. Members of the police force, defense force, fire brigade, and prison guards may not organize or join unions.

Enforcement of labor laws was weak. There was no information on the adequacy of enforcement resources. Fines varied widely by case and were not sufficient to deter violations. Administrative and judicial procedures were subject to lengthy delays and appeals. The government did not provide updated statistics during the year. By law labor disputes must first be filed with the Ministry of Labor and National Insurance, and if not resolved, they are transferred to an industrial tribunal, which determines penalties (fines) and remedies, up to a maximum of 26 weeks of an employee's pay. The tribunal's decision is final and can be appealed in court only on a strict question of law. Authorities reported a case backlog of up to three years at the tribunal.

The government generally respected freedom of association and the right to collective bargaining, and most employers in the private sector did as well. There were reports that some employers utilized individual contracts instead of collective bargaining. Workers occasionally filed disputes with the authorities involving "union-busting" charges, specifically in the financial services sector. During the year two such cases arose and were resolved in a timely manner through conciliation.

b. Prohibition of Forced or Compulsory Labor

The law prohibits all forms of forced or compulsory labor.

The government did not always effectively enforce applicable law. Although the Ministry of Labor and National Insurance received no reports of forced labor during the year, local NGOs noted that exploited workers often did not report their circumstances to government officials due to fear of deportation and lack of education about available resources. There was no information on the adequacy of resources, inspections, and remediation. Penalties for forced labor range from three to 10 years' imprisonment and were sufficiently stringent to deter violations.

Undocumented migrants were vulnerable to forced labor, especially in domestic servitude and in the agriculture sector. There were reports that noncitizen laborers, often of Haitian origin, were vulnerable to forced labor and suffered abuses at the hands of their employers, who were responsible for endorsing their work permits on an annual basis. Specifically, local sources indicated that employers reportedly obtained $1,000 work permits for noncitizen employees and then required them to "work off" the permit fee over the course of their employment or otherwise risk losing the permit and their ability to work legally within the country.

Also see the Department of State's *Trafficking in Persons Report* at www.state.gov/j/tip/rls/tiprpt/.

c. Prohibition of Child Labor and Minimum Age for Employment

The law prohibits the employment of children under age 14 for industrial work or work during school hours. Children under age 16 may not work at night. Children between the ages 14 and 18 may work outside of school hours under the following conditions: in a school day, for not more than three hours; in a school week, for not more than 24 hours; in a nonschool day, for not more than eight hours; in a nonschool week, for not more than 40 hours. The law prohibits persons younger than age 18 from engaging in dangerous work, including construction, mining, and road building. There was no legal minimum age for employment in other sectors. Occupational health and safety restrictions apply to all younger workers. Grocery stores frequently violated labor laws by employing "package boys," some as young as 13, outside of legal working hours.

The government made efforts to enforce the law, with labor inspectors proactively sent to stores and businesses on a regular basis, but resource constraints limited their effectiveness. The Ministry of Labor and National Insurance reported no severe violations of child labor laws, although inspectors reported several instances of children working in small merchant businesses or excess hours in grocery stores. The penalty for violations of child labor law is a fine between $1,000 and $1,500. This punitive action was sufficient to deter violations.

d. Discrimination with Respect to Employment and Occupation

The law prohibits discrimination in employment based on race, color, national origin, creed, sex, marital status, political opinion, age, HIV status, or disability, but not in regard to language, sexual orientation and/or gender identity, religion, or social status. The government did not effectively enforce the law, and while the law allows victims to sue for damages, many citizens were unable to avail themselves of this remedy due to poor availability of legal representation and the ability of wealthy defendants to drag out the process in courts. Discrimination in employment and occupation occurred with respect to persons with HIV/AIDS (see section 6). Foreign migrant workers consistently received legal protections.

e. Acceptable Conditions of Work

In July 2015 the Ministry of Labor and National Insurance raised the minimum wage from $4.00 to $5.25 per hour. In 2013 the official poverty level was adjusted to $4,247 a year. In June 2015 the government appointed a National Tripartite Council to implement the statutory provisions of International Labor Organization Convention 144 and ensure effective consultation among employers, government, and workers.

The law provides for a 40-hour workweek, a 24-hour rest period, and time-and-a-half payment for hours worked beyond the standard workweek. The law stipulates paid annual holidays and prohibits compulsory overtime. The law does not place a cap on overtime. The government set health and safety standards appropriate to the industries. According to the Ministry of Labor and National Insurance, the law protects all workers, including migrant workers, in areas including wages, working hours, working conditions, and occupational and safety standards. Workers do not have the right to refuse to work under hazardous conditions, and legal standards do not cover undocumented and informal economy workers.

The ministry is responsible for enforcing labor laws, including the minimum wage, and fielded a team of 16 inspectors that conducted onsite visits to enforce occupational health and safety standards and investigate employee concerns and complaints, although inspections occurred infrequently. The ministry generally announced inspection visits in advance, and employers generally cooperated with inspectors to implement safety standards. It was uncertain whether these inspections were effective in enforcing health and safety standards. The government did not levy fines for noncompliance but occasionally forced a work stoppage. Such penalties were not sufficiently stringent to deter violations. Working conditions varied, and mold was a problem in schools and government facilities.

www.ingramcontent.com/pod-product-compliance
Lightning Source LLC
Chambersburg PA
CBHW080822280726
48660CB00018B/3569